Pet Parakeets

Cecelia H. Brannon

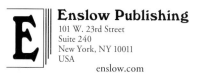

Enslow Publishing
101 W. 23rd Street
Suite 240
New York, NY 10011
USA

enslow.com

Published in 2017 by Enslow Publishing, LLC.
101 W. 23rd Street, Suite 240, New York, NY 10011

Library of Congress Cataloging-in-Publication Data

Names: Brannon, Cecelia H., author.
Title: Pet parakeets / Cecelia H. Brannon.
Description: New York, NY : Enslow Publishing, 2017. | Series: All about pets | Audience: Age 4-up. | Audience: Pre-school, excluding K. | Includes bibliographical references and index.
Identifiers: LCCN 2015045455| ISBN 9780766076075 (library bound) | ISBN 9780766076358 (pbk.) | ISBN 9780766075917 (6-pack)
Subjects: LCSH: Parrots--Juvenile literature. | CYAC: Parakeets.
Classification: LCC SF473.P3 B66 2017 | DDC 636.6/865--dc23
LC record available at http://lccn.loc.gov/2015045455

Printed in Malaysia

To Our Readers: We have done our best to make sure all website addresses in this book were active and appropriate when we went to press. However, the author and the publisher have no control over and assume no liability for the material available on those websites or on any websites they may link to. Any comments or suggestions can be sent by e-mail to customerservice@enslow.com.

Photos Credits: Cover, Africa Studio/Shutterstock.com; p. 1 Eudyptula/Shutterstock.com; pp. 3 (center), 12 waldru/Shutterstock.com; pp. 3 (right), 10 itonggg/Shutterstock.com; p. 4–5 Lusyaya/iStock/Thinkstock; pp. 3 (left), 6 iStock.com/FOTOGRAFIA INC; p. 8 Zurijeta/iStock/Thinkstock; p. 14 iStock.com/EVAfotografie; p. 16 CrystalMage/Shutterstock.com; p. 18 Paul Bricknell/Dorling Kindersley/Getty Images; p. 20 AnBra/iStock/Thinkstock; p. 22 imagenavi/Getty Images.

Contents

Words to Know

beak   cage   wings

A parakeet is a kind of bird. Parakeets are bright and colorful. People like to keep them as pets.

Parakeets are very smart. They can sing, whistle, and even talk!

Parakeets can learn tricks. You can teach a parakeet to sit on your finger!

A parakeet has a long tail, a sharp beak, and wings.

A parakeet lives in a large cage. It needs room to move, but it shouldn't be able to fly away!

You must let your parakeet out of its cage every now and then. This is how it exercises. But be sure the windows are closed!

A parakeet's cage must be cleaned every week. You must put fresh paper down on the bottom.

Parakeets love the water. Just like you, they take baths to stay clean.

Parakeets eat seeds, nuts, and sometimes fruit.

If you take good care of your parakeet, it will be your friend for a long time!

Read More

Alderton, David. *How to Look After Your Budgie.* London: Armadillo, 2014.

Thomas, Isabel. *Beaky's Guide to Caring for Your Bird.* Portsmouth, NH: Heinemann, 2014.

Websites

National Wildlife Federation
  nwf.org/Kids/Ranger-Rick/Animals/Birds/Budgies.aspx

Birdtricks.com
  birdtricks.com/Parakeet/parakeet-facts.html

Index

Guided Reading Level: C
Guided Reading Leveling System is based on the guidelines recommended by Fountas and Pinnell.

Word Count: 154